CELEBRATING
CHRISTMAS
TOGETHER

Nativity and Three Kings Plays
with stories and songs

Estelle Bryer and Janni Nicol
illustrated by Janni Nicol

Hawthorn Press

Celebrating Christmas together © Copyright 2001 Estelle Bryer and Janni Nicol

Estelle Bryer and Janni Nicol are hereby identified as authors of this work in accordance with Section 77 of the Copyright, Designs and Patent Act, 1988. They assert and give notice of their moral right under this Act.

Published by Hawthorn Press, Hawthorn House, 1 Lansdown Lane, Stroud, Gloucestershire, GL5 1BJ, UK
Tel: (01453) 757040 Fax: (01453) 751138
info@hawthornpress.com
www.hawthornpress.com

Cover illustration by Marije Rowling
Illustrations by Janni Nicol
Cover design by Hawthorn Press
Typesetting by Hawthorn Press, Stroud, Glos.
Printed in the UK by The Cromwell Press. Trowbridge, Wilts.

Grateful acknowledgment to:

Every effort has been made to trace the ownership of all copyrighted material. If any omission has been made, please bring this to the publisher's attention so that proper acknowledgment may be given in future editions.

British Library Cataloguing in Publication Data applied for

ISBN 1 903458 20 X

Contents

This book is dedicated to Janine Hurner without whom
the plays would never have come about.

Foreword

by Winny Mossman

Christmas: a time of goodwill, celebration with family and friends – and also of commercialism and greedy excess! There are few people whose joyful expectation is not tinged with dread, for whom Christmas is not a potentially fraught time of difficult family relationships, financial worries and other pitfalls.

But many of us also have memories of magical Christmases back in early childhood, when life seemed simpler and the light that shone from the stable filled the world around us with a sense of wonder. This book is an inspiration for adults who want to create such memories for their children.

As a kindergarten teacher in a Steiner Waldorf School I feel privileged to share Christmas with young children and their parents. During the four weeks of Advent it is possible to redress the balance, turn the 'getting' into 'giving', the 'shopping' into 'making', to prepare our hearts and homes for shared celebration, whether we believe in the religious significance of Christmas or simply want to give and share with family and friends. Estelle and Janni's lovely and practical book will prove an invaluable companion on this journey.

In our kindergarten, preparation starts with the Festival of the Advent Garden, when each child's lit candle adds to a crescendo of light that glitters on crystals in the darkness of a moss and fir spiral. Through Advent the classroom slowly fills with greenery and stars, and the 'stained glass tissue' pictures of the Advent calendar shine in the classroom window. Much secret making and baking fill the children's thoughts and hearts with the joy of giving, and their senses with the warm smells of cinnamon and spice. Our preparation culminates in the end of term Christmas Festival where we share our 'play' with the parents and give them the presents we've worked so hard to make.

At home too, Advent Sundays can be filled with activities such as making an Advent Wreath, Christmas card making, biscuit baking, and candle dipping – even nicer when shared with friends. The Angel Advent Calendar from this book, Christmas Carols and a candle-lit story time can mark the end of each day leading up to Christmas Eve and the excitement of Christmas and Boxing Day, filled with giving and receiving presents and sharing good things to eat and drink! After Boxing Day the twelve Holy Nights carry us through the special quiet point of the year to Three Kings' Day. Acting out Estelle and Janni's Nativity and Three Kings Play during this time will involve all the family and their friends, young and old alike, in creating a warm feeling of community.

On Three Kings' Day small children particularly can take real comfort from the image of the Three Kings carrying away the Christmas Tree (while they are asleep!); and for older children the last lighting of the tree before helping to undress it, sharing a story and singing Carols together, brings Christmas to an end and at the same time opens the door to the Epiphany period, with its powerful images of mutual help and guarding against evil.

Estelle and Janni's book is a rich source of material for teachers and parents looking for new ways to celebrate Christmas and Epiphany. It will inspire people everywhere to create – each in their own way – a festival that truly encompasses the spirit of Christmas for the children in their care, and rekindles the sense of wonder so easily lost in our busy lives.

Winny Mossman
Kindergarten, Bristol Waldorf School

Introduction

This verse form of the nativity story was written in 1965 for the kindergarten of the Constantia Waldorf School, Cape Town, South Africa, as a play to be performed by children for their parents.

Over the years it has barely changed as we have found it difficult to improve on, and it has now become a tradition in our schools.

As a PLAY small or large groups can perform it both at school and at home. It has been performed by as many as 65 children, where each class contributed a portion of the play to the final performance, with a narrator and orchestra. It also works well when parents or students perform it for the children's Christmas festival.

As a STORY in verse form it stands complete in its own right, to be read by teachers and parents to the children. It can also accompany the build-up of a NATIVITY SCENE to be enacted by the various doll figures. Told on Christmas Eve in front of a candle-lit nativity scene, the story brings a reverent mood to the celebrations, contributing to a lifelong memory of the event.

As a PUPPET PLAY it works well too, using hand puppets, marionettes or tabletop doll figures.

The CHRISTMAS STORIES can be told at any time, adding richness to celebrations over the Christmas period in either Northern or Southern hemispheres.

Creating the Nativity Scene

Because young children learn through active participation, it is best to let them help build up a small nativity scene, for this adds to the Advent mood of anticipation.

In the Southern hemisphere where Christmas usually falls in the middle of the summer holidays, the right mood may still be maintained through slowly building up this scene at home, singing Christmas songs and making presents together as a family. (A handmade present, no matter how primitive, is often more lovely to receive than a bought one. And gives the giver more pleasure too!).

If the children perform the play, then its characters can simultaneously be added to the small nativity scene. If the play is read purely as a STORY, then the nativity scene can be slowly built up to accompany the reading, which can take place repeatedly, preferably in the evening, during Advent as well as on Christmas Eve; and also on the twelve nights between Christmas and Epiphany (Three Kings Day).

The nativity story begins only after the first Advent Sunday, and that is when one can begin to build the scene. It progresses slowly over the four weeks leading up to Christmas. If the scene is built up at school, then it can be done all at once. If school finishes long before Christmas it is not necessary to introduce all the characters, for they can still be travelling 'towards' the stable. This increases the children's sense of anticipation.

An advent calendar in the form of an angel carrying the baby towards the stable can be introduced on the first Advent Sunday, the angel travelling a little closer each day to arrive above the

stable on Christmas Eve. The baby only appears in the manger
on Christmas morning.

Instructions for making
the Advent Calendar are
in Appendix 3.

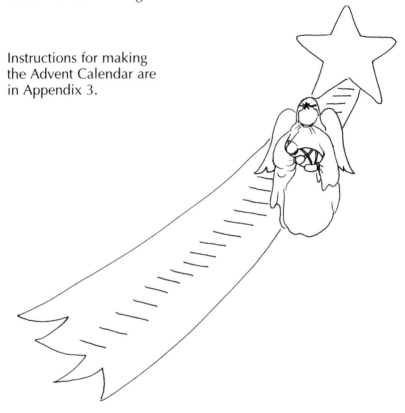

(The following instructions are for setting up the scene at home.)

THE SCENE

On the first Advent Sunday drape a soft blue cloth in an alcove,
over a table or even on a windowsill. This forms the backdrop
on which the stars can be hung. In the first two weeks, together
with the children, slowly add rocks and semi-precious stones,
moss, grasses, little fir trees (branches), pine cones, plants and
flowers (dried or in little bunches of fresh flowers in vases). The

stable can be created from bark or wood; or a box, cut out, painted and draped with material can be used.

In the third week animals come into the landscape, sheep in the field, a squirrel in the trees, a rabbit sitting in the grass, a little mouse hiding in the stable, a spider in a corner, a pigeon on the roof and an ox quietly sleeping.

In the fourth week the shepherds arrive in the fields, to look after their sheep, and Mary, Joseph and the donkey begin their journey through the landscape (or even from across the room) towards the stable.

Only on Christmas Eve do they arrive at the stable. On Christmas morning the angel who has brought the baby appears. With much delight the children will also discover the 'special' baby lying in the manger.

(If the story is told in its entirety before Christmas Eve, another baby can substitute until the 'special' one appears.)

The story can be retold each evening during the Holy Nights, accompanied by the lighting of candles and carol singing. The children love nothing more than to move the figures as the story is told. Children learn through imitation, so if the adult moves/acts them with the necessary reverence and gentleness the first time, the children will imitate this thereafter.

Animals can appear as the stories from 'The Animals in the Stable' are told, and the Three Kings begin their journey across the room to arrive at the stable on the 6th January.

After the Three Kings have left the stable, one can explain that now Mary, Joseph, the baby and the donkey have to go on their journey to Egypt. They say 'Goodbye and thank you' to the animals, the rosebush etc., and the stable. And now everything can go to sleep until next Christmas.

The stable and contents can then be packed carefully into boxes, also all the decorations from the tree and the rest of the house. The children can help with this if they wish. The Christmas tree is also removed (though preferably at night while the children are asleep).

(See Appendix 2 for instructions for making the figures.)

THE NATIVITY PLAY

It is possible for this play to be performed in many different ways, with children aged three upwards. It can be performed in its simplest format for small groups of children in families; also with whole school groups in a Christmas performance, with each class contributing one section. Adults can also perform it for children.

Because the story is narrated, young children feel secure in miming and only speaking their parts if they wish to. Children and adults may sing together. (The audience may join in if desired, particularly in the last song.)

Depending on the number of children participating, whole sequences may be left out or added.

Songs may be changed or left out. Traditional songs, which are well known to parents and children may be used and repeated.

Throughout the preparation/rehearsal period (which can be from one to two or more weeks), the adult should act the story together with the children, as young children learn through imitation and not through instruction. The important thing is the sheer enjoyment of it and NOT the end result.

Children take it in turns to be the different parts, and costumes are added gradually to enhance the mood of anticipation.

If the adult softly sings the songs during daily activities and present-making, the children will join in: not only will they learn the songs quickly but the whole atmosphere of preparation will benefit too.

A doll may reverently be used as 'the baby' but for the actual performance a special, soft baby doll – delicately wrapped in a pale colour – should be introduced.

It is preferable that all stories told during this period have a Christmas theme and that activities also be Christmas orientated – for instance the making of costumes for the play, presents, or decorations.

Gentle reverence and respect help engender the right Christmas mood.

SETTING THE SCENE FOR THE PERFORMANCE

The mood is enhanced if the room is semi-dark, lit only with a few candles. A real Christmas tree could stand safely to one side (with candles lit during the play.)

The stable can be simply made and laid out as in fig 1.

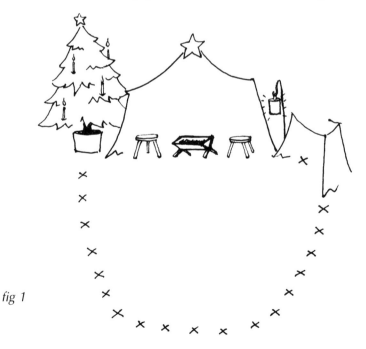

fig 1

CHARACTERS (in order of appearance)

Star Angel
Ox
Farmer
3 Shepherds
Baby Angel
Stars/angels
Bunnies
Cuckoo and pigeon
Rosebush and fairies
Gnomes
Kings
Mary
Joseph and the donkey

Children enter in the above sequence. The Star Angel goes to stand next to the stable together with the Ox (on hands and knees). The Baby Angel carries the baby, the Farmer carries the lit lantern, Shepherds and Kings carry gifts and the Stars carry their stars. They put their gifts, stars and bells under their chairs.

Song for entrance:
PEOPLE LOOK EAST
or
O COME ALL YE CHILDREN.

When all the children are seated Mary, Joseph and the Donkey (on hands and knees) enter and the narration begins.

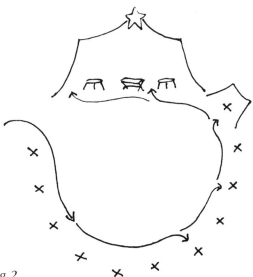

fig 2

1 NATIVITY

Mary, Joseph and the donkey make their way, as in the diagram, to the Farmer. Joseph knocks on the floor with his staff. The Farmer indicates the stable then leads them there, gives them the lantern, bows and then returns to his place. Joseph hangs up the lantern and they sit. Mary crosses her arms over her breast.

'Twas on a deep and silent night
The earth in darkness lay,
When Mary mild and Joseph
To Bethlehem made their way.

From house to house they wandered
No one had room for them,
Till at a little farmhouse
They knocked again.

The farmer came and kindly said:
'No room is free today,
But in this little stable here
Gladly you may stay.'

He led them to the stable
Gave them his lantern light,
He bowed before the maiden
And said 'Good night'.

And Joseph said 'God bless you!'
The donkey went 'He – Haw!'
The ox went 'Moo' and bowed his head
And both were munching straw.

And all around the stable
The earth was very quiet,
The whole world seemed to listen
It was the holy night.

2 ANGEL

Soft music could accompany the entry of the Baby Angel. She walks slowly carrying the baby gently, circles the play area, then stands close to Mary who sits with her arms crossed over her breast. Mary lifts up her arms to receive the baby, which the Angel gently places into her hands. She brings it slowly down, folds her cloak around it and cradles it. The Angel can either remain with Mary or return to her chair. If the whole sequence is done silently to music, then the verse 'It stopped above the stable...light' may be omitted.

During the singing of SILENT NIGHT the candles on the Christmas tree and elsewhere may be lit.

During the last verse the Ox and Donkey could 'breathe' on the baby to keep it warm.

Hush, in the silent darkness
I heard an angel's wing,
A golden star from heaven
Came journeying

Soft music – e.g. lyre

It stopped above the stable
To shine with radiance bright
And there to Mother Mary
Was born the child of light.

Song: SILENT NIGHT (while lighting the candles on the Christmas tree)

When Joseph saw the child was born
And had no place to rest,
He made him in the manger
A soft little nest.

**And Mary laid the baby down
And covered his tiny form.
The ox and donkey nestled close
To keep him warm.**

Song: AWAY IN A MANGER

3 SHEPHERDS

Shepherds place their gifts in the centre of the play area, then dance and skip around in the circle to the song. They lie down and the Star Angel fetches the Angels (Stars) who carry bells and circle around the shepherds during the song DING DONG MERRILY ON HIGH. They then return to their seats and the Star Angel leads the shepherds 'through the hills' (space permitting – see fig 3) to the stable during the song O COME ALL YE CHILDREN. They return to their seats in the same way and the Star Angel remains beside the stable.

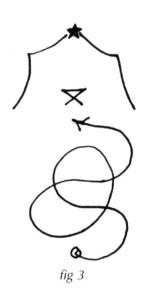

fig 3

**Now who was awake
In the night so deep?
Three shepherds were playing
While watching their sheep.**

Song: THREE SHEPHERD BOYS OF THE HILLS ARE WE

**The shepherds grew tired,
Lay down by their sheep,
No sooner they lay
They were fast asleep.**

And lo, there appeared a wond'rous light
And angels sang in the holy night...with all their might...

Song: DING DONG MERRILY ON HIGH

The shepherds awoke and jumped to their feet,
'Come, let us go the child to greet.'
'I'll bring a fur to deck his bed.'
'I'll bring some wool, to rest his head.'
'I'll bring my lamb as white as snow
Now come, let us go, let us go.'

Song: O COME, ALL YE CHILDREN

They came to the stable and knocked at the door
And found baby Jesus on hay and on straw.
Knelt down before the manger low
And gently rocked him to and fro.

Song: LITTLE JESUS SWEETLY SLEEP (1st verse)

And when they had rocked the little child,
They gave their gifts to Mary mild,
And bowed and said 'Goodbye' to all,
And softly left the little stall.

Song: AWAY IN A MANGER

4 EXTRAS

And the beasts of the field
And the birds of the air
All brought their gifts
To the child so fair

(The following lines and songs are dramatised)

BUNNIES

They hop to the play area and mime the song, they then hop to the stable and take their 'softest fluff' from over their hearts, make a little ball and throw it into the crib. They hop back to their places.

Song: SEE THE LITTLE BUNNIES SLEEPING

They waggled their ears
And said their prayers
Then took their softest fluff,
And for the little Jesus child
They made a little muff.

End of bunny song (Hop little bunny)

CUCKOO AND PIGEON

They dance the words of the song in the play area one at a time.

From out of the woods did a cuckoo fly, coo-coo
He came to the manger with joyful cry, coo-coo
He hopped, he curtsied, round he flew,
And loud his jubilation grew, coo-coo, coo-coo, coo-coo.

A pigeon flew over from Galilee, froo-croo,
He strutted and coo'd and was full of glee, froo-croo.
He sang with jewelled wings unfurled
His joy that Christ was in the world.
Froo-croo, froo-croo, froo-croo.

ROSEBUSH/FAIRIES

The Rosebush kneels on the floor with a basket of red paper roses in front of her. She gives each Fairy a rose which they place in the crib after twirling and dancing to the song I'VE ROCKED MY SWEET BABE. (fig 4)

A little rose bush sadly smiled,
Her roses she would give the child,
She could not move, her roots were stuck
Please … who could help, her roses
pluck?

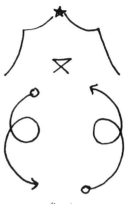

On golden shoes the fairies pranced
And for the child of love they danced,
They brought to him their roses sweet
And placed them round his tiny feet.

Song: I'VE ROCKED MY SWEET BABE IN
HIS CRADLE TO REST

fig 4

All kissed the little child good-bye.
They curtsied and away did fly.

GNOMES

They follow each other in a line to the play area while acting
out the song and verse, they then go to the stable where they
'give their crystals' to Mary and Joseph and mime the song.

(Speak in strong rhythms, stressing each syllable)

Bearded little mountain gnomes
Then came out of their mountain homes.

Song: WE ARE THE CLEVER LITTLE GNOMES

Hammer, hammer, hammer bright
The crystals clear of starry light.

(repeat above while 'hammering' in rhythm)

They marched in through the stable door
And laid their gifts upon the floor.

Song: LITTLE JESUS SWEETLY SLEEP – (2nd verse)

Politely bowed the little gnomes
And went back to their mountain homes.
Their little sacks upon their backs
With clip-a-dee-clap and nick-a-dee nack.

Repeat gnome song

5   STARS

One of the stars acts the song and the rest of the stars join in when indicated. They 'twinkle' their stars above their heads.

Outside the little stable
From up in heaven high
A little shining golden star
Came twinkling through the sky.

Song: (to act)

From heaven's arc so high
A little light draws nigh,
Stops to stare, stands quite near,
Wonders what is happening there.

The mother with her baby
Calls the light in gaily,
'Come in here, come in here,
Light us with your radiance clear.'

Then all the lights divine,
Bring their golden shine,
And they bow, deep and low,
Bringing him their heavenly glow.

Song: TWINKLE, TWINKLE LITTLE STAR

....

You may wish to end the play here, especially if you are

intending to perform the Three Kings Play later, at Epiphany. If
so, the stars can stand in an arc on either side of the stable for
the last song. Otherwise they return to their seats.

....

6 KINGS

*They mime the words, then take their gifts and regally follow the
Star Angel who leads them to the stable during the song WE
THREE KINGS. They kneel one at a time to present their gifts
and say their lines.*

Order of kings: Red King, Blue King, Green King.

*They return to their seats during the repeat singing of WE THREE
KINGS.*

Three noble kings from far-off lands,
Three Magi wond'rous wise,
Were gazing at the stars that night
A-glittering in the skies.

And as they looked a shining star
Appeared in heaven's dome
To lead them to the newborn king
And all three left their homes.

Song: WE THREE KINGS OF ORIENT ARE

At last the shining star did rest
Over the stable door,
The three kings stood there silently
Then knelt down on the floor.

'Greetings to thee, child so fair,
Gold I bring to thee.'
'Greetings to thee, child so rare,
Frankincense I bring to thee.'

'Greetings to thee, child so dear,
Healing myrrh I bring to thee.'

They bowed before the little child
And to his mother Mary mild
Then quietly left the stall.

Song: WE THREE KINGS OF ORIENT ARE

7 ENDING

*This verse may end the entire play at any stage. The children
stand at each side of the stable during the song DING DONG
MERRILY ON HIGH, all singing together.*

And the flower bells all rang with joy
Praising the birth of the heavenly boy.

Song: DING DONG MERRILY ON HIGH

fig 5

THE THREE KINGS PLAY

This play is generally performed during Epiphany (on and after Three Kings' Day on the 6th January). This creates a sense of continuity for the children, to take the Christmas theme over the holidays. The children love to be involved in the making of the costumes, gifts and telescopes for the Kings to use.

The play can be continued for at least two weeks, the children having the opportunity once again to act each part in turn. It is possible to have more than one servant, or even to introduce camels, horses or more stars into the play.

We have also found that the children enjoy watching each other and it is not always necessary for each one to participate every day or to perform for adults. They simply take pleasure in doing it themselves.

CHARACTERS (in order of appearance)

Star
Mary holding baby
Ox
Donkey
Joseph
Blue King and Servant
Red King and Servant
Green King and Servant
(Extra stars if needed)

All enter singing STAR HIGH BABY LOW

Star high, baby low
Twixt the two, wise men go,

**Find the baby, greet the star,
King of all things near and far.**

*All sit. Mary, Joseph, Ox, Donkey in the stable, the Star(s) stand
outside. The Kings sit in their 'kingdoms' on 'thrones', covered in
appropriate coloured materials.*

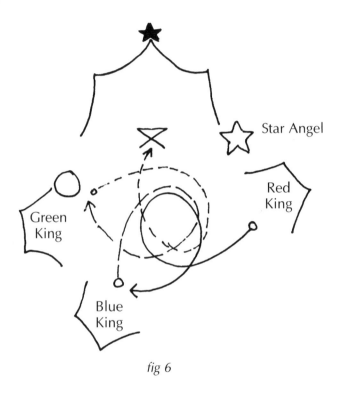

Star Angel

Red
King

Green
King

Blue
King

fig 6

RED KING: *stands, takes his cup and goes to the central play
area. He mimes the words and looks into the cup which he
holds towards Mary ('a crown'). She beckons to him, 'come to
me'. When this part has finished he calls to his servant to bring
his red cloak, which he fastens around the king's neck. The
servant then brings him his gold box and takes the gold cup.
They sit down. He puts the gold cup under his seat.*

In a beautiful golden castle,
Lived King Melchior, good and wise,
He had a tall, tall tower
From where he'd see star skies.

A golden cup he always took,
In which the stars reflected.
One night he stood there all amazed
At what he'd not expected.

A crown of stars it showed him
Around a mother's hair
With cloak as blue as heaven
Holding her child so fair.

'Come to me,' she seemed to say,
'A star shall guide you on your way'.

He beckons to the servant

'Go bring my camels and red cloak,
I'll take my gold as gift.
Now come my men, for we must go
On our camels swift.'

Song: STAR HIGH

BLUE KING: *stands and goes to the centre. He holds the bowl (adult lights incense?) Holds bowl up. Repeat as for Red King.*

In a distant far-off land
There lived another king
Who had a hall with glassy roof
To let the starlight in.

King Balthazar lit frankincense
From which the smoke curled high,
And in it he saw pictures
Ascending to the sky.

A crown of stars it showed him
Around a mother's hair
With cloak as blue as heaven
Holding her child so fair.

'Come to me,' she seemed to say
'The star shall guide you on your way'.

He beckons to his servant

'Go bring my camels and blue cloak,
And frankincense as gift.
Now come my men for we must go,
On our camels swift.'

Song: STAR HIGH

GREEN KING: *stands (there is a cloth 'well' next to the chair in the 'kingdom'). The king kneels next to the well. Repeat as for other kings.*

King Caspar lived in a far-off land
Great stories he could tell
From what the starry skies sang down
Reflected in his well.

One night he knelt beside the well
To hear the heaven's story
But in the water deep and blue
He saw a sight of glory.

A crown of stars it showed him
Around a mother's hair
With cloak as blue as heaven
Holding her child so fair.

'Come to me,' she seemed to say
'The star shall guide you on your way'.

He beckons to his servant

'Go, bring my camels and green cloak
And myrrh as healing gift.
Come, my men, for we must go
On our camels swift.'

*All the kings and their servants stand up and walk in different
directions behind and around their chairs to meet in central play
area while at the same time the star comes to meet them in the
central area. Then the star leads them and during the chorus
guides them to the stable. All three kings kneel and remove their
crowns, placing them on the ground. The servants wait behind
them holding the gifts. One king at a time stands to give his gift,
which he takes from his servant. Then all stand and bow,
replace their crowns, and leave the stable. The servants follow.
During the last song they return to their chairs.*

Song: WE THREE KINGS OF ORIENT ARE (first verse)

The kings they journeyed through the land
Until at last they met
Beneath the star that guided them.
Then, together, onward set.

Song: WE THREE KINGS OF ORIENT ARE (chorus)

At last the shining star did rest
Over the stable door
The three kings stood there silently,
Then knelt upon the floor.

For lo, before them was the sight
The stars had sparkled down,
The mother crowned with stars aglow
The child who wore a crown.

'Greetings to thee, child so fair,
Gold I bring to thee.'

'Greetings to thee, child so rare,
Frankincense I bring to thee.'

'Greetings to thee, child so dear
Healing myrrh I bring to thee.'

They bowed before the little child,
Before the mother Mary mild,
Then quietly left the stall.

Song: WE THREE KINGS OF ORIENT ARE

The Story of the Crystal

A long, long time ago, Mother Earth sat deep in her cave under the earth, singing to the little seeds that were sleeping through the winter. Each year it seemed to grow darker within the earth, so she called the little gnomes to her and asked, 'Are you polishing the stones and crystals, for they are losing their light?' The gnomes agreed, for no matter how much they polished the stones, these grew duller and darker.

'We will go and find out why the light is leaving the earth,' said the gnomes; and they chose some beautiful but dull crystals, which they put in their sacks, and with their sacks on their backs they set off on their long journey.

For many months they travelled and still they could not find out where the light had gone. One night, tired and weary, they settled in a field with some sheep. The stars twinkled in the heavens and one, which was bigger and brighter than the others, shone so brightly that the earth was lit as if it were daylight. The gnomes thought that if only they could capture a little bit of the light from that beautiful star it would be enough to make all the stones and crystals shine within the earth, so they set off once again with their sacks on their backs, this time following the great star.

As they walked they looked up to see angels flying in the heavens, singing 'Gloria! Gloria!' Their steps quickened and soon they came to a small stable at the back of the inn. From within there came a radiant light spilling out of the doorway. The gnomes stood in the shadows outside watching.

Some shepherds went in bearing gifts and when they came out

again their faces were filled with joy and happiness. 'We have
only dull crystals in our sacks,' said the gnomes sadly, 'but we
would love to see what this light is that shines so brightly on this
dark night.'

So quietly they went inside the stable. They saw an ox and an
ass standing in the corner, and a father stoking the fire. A mother
sat near a manger. She smiled at the gnomes and held out her
hand. 'Come closer,' she said, 'come and greet my son.' The
gnomes took out their dull crystals and held them out to the
baby so that he could see the shapes within ... and lo... the
crystals began to shine and sparkle again, and as they caught the
light they sent out rays which filled the air with different colours,
and the baby laughed with delight.

One gnome turned to the beautiful mother and asked, 'Who is
this special child who makes everything shine again?' And she
answered: 'This is the baby Jesus whom God has given to us as
a gift, filled with love for the earth and all who live on it. His
love will make the earth sing and shine again. Take your crystals
back into the earth, little gnomes, with the love which you have
felt here tonight, and tell all you see about God's gift to the
earth.'

The little gnomes bowed to the mother and the baby and with
joy in their hearts and the crystals shining brightly to guide their
way, they set off home.

The Shepherd Boy and the Lamb

A little shepherd boy lay sleeping with the shepherds in the fields one night. The fire warmed them and the sparks from the flames flew up into the night sky like the stars shining so brightly in the heavens. As he lay sleeping he dreamed that he heard bells ringing and angels singing – and he awoke with a start. The fire had died down and all was quiet, except for the occasional bleating of the sheep as they settled down to sleep. The little shepherd cuddled close to his little lamb, nestling into the warm wool, and went back to sleep.

In the morning when he awoke, he went with his lamb to the stream to drink and wash his face. When he had washed he found that his lamb had disappeared. 'Lambie, Lambie, where are you?' called the shepherd boy, and he began to search everywhere for him, running down the stream, over the fields, through bushes and grass, until he came to a forest. 'He must have gone in here,' he said and wandered further and further into the forest and away from the other shepherds, still calling his lamb.

Before he knew what had happened he felt himself falling... crashing though leaves and branches until he landed with a bump on the ground at the bottom of a hole. He jumped up, and, relieved to find he wasn't hurt, he brushed himself off, but no matter how hard he tried to climb out of the hole he couldn't find a way up, so he sat down on a root and began to cry. Suddenly he heard a tinkling sound. 'Lambie, is that you?' he called, and the little lamb's furry face appeared above the hole. 'Please go back to the field and fetch the shepherds to help me out of this hole,' he cried. The lamb went bouncing off, the bell tinkling softer and softer as he went further and further away.

The sun went down and the stars appeared through the trees, burning so brightly in the heavens that it was like daylight shining into his deep hole. Suddenly he did not feel afraid, and as the shepherd boy watched the stars, he heard the sound of bells ringing. It was as if all the heavens were filled with music... *'Ding dong merrily on high, in heaven the bells are ringing...Gloria...'* he sang loudly, joining in with the heavenly singing.

Suddenly the bells became louder and louder, and he looked up to see his lamb, the sheep and the shepherds, looking down at him. His lamb had fetched them after all! They pulled him up out of the deep hole, and wrapping him in fur to keep him warm, they carried him back to the fire, his lamb running happily behind him.

'Did you hear the heavenly bells ringing, the angels singing, and why are the stars shining so brightly?' asked the boy. The old shepherd answered, 'Tonight is special, for a heavenly shining child has been born to bring joy and love to the earth. When we have had some food and drink, we will go to find him, the angels have told us to follow that bright star you can see over there.'

So they ate and drank by the fire. And before they set off to follow the star, the old shepherd gave the little boy a gift too... a little bell to hang around his neck. 'Here,' he said, 'now you will not get lost again, for wherever you go we will hear your little bell ringing, and we will find you, just as your little lamb found you tonight.' The little shepherd boy thanked the shepherd, and each shepherd took a gift for the child. One took some fur to deck his bed, another took some wool to rest his head, and the little shepherd took his lamb as white as snow. As they walked over the fields following the bright star, he could hear his little golden bell tinkling as brightly and sweetly as the bells ringing in the heavens.

And in a little stable they found the child of light, and gave their gifts to his Mother Mary, who wore a mantle as blue as the heavens. They knelt before the little manger where the child lay, and saw that truly he was the most beautiful child in all the world.

And the air was full of the sound of angels singing GLORIA to all mankind.

The Animals in the Stable

It was not only the ox and donkey who were present in the stable at the birth of the Jesus child, but a little dove cooed where it slept inside on the beams of the old roof. In the corner sat a fat spider in the middle of her web. A little mouse squeaked in its hole and polished its tiny nose with its paws.

THE OX AND THE DONKEY

Near the manger where the mother had placed her baby lay the ox and the donkey. From where they lay they could see the baby in the manger surrounded in a halo of light. 'Oh, oh!' brayed the donkey softly to the ox, 'who would have thought that when I brought the maiden here on my back, a little baby would be sleeping in the manger out of which we are supposed to eat. There lies the poor little child in the hay; he should lie in the best and softest cradle in the world with a warm blanket to keep him warm. I would rather have taken him to the finest house in the world, for do you not see how beautiful the child is?'

'Moo,' answered the ox, 'please do not let us eat of the hay, we can go hungry for a while so that the child can have a comfortable bed to lie in; tomorrow we can eat the grass outside the stable, we will leave the hay to keep the little one warm.' And they settled down and breathed softly over the child to warm the air around him.

THE DOVES

The doves on the beams of the stable began to coo: 'Through the window in the roof the sky is shining with glorious light and there is movement there too, look, there are flocks of angels flying like birds – oh listen how they are singing, let us join in their song, but quietly, for we do not want to waken the little child'. And the doves cooed gently, a little lullaby for the baby boy.

THE SPIDER

Sitting comfortably in her web, a big fat spider was woken up by the cooing of the doves. Inquisitively she crept out and walked over the beam. Fortunately it was too dark for the doves to see her or she would have been pecked up! She scurried quickly to the window for she was curious to see what the doves had been cooing about, and when she saw the angels she called out to them 'Please give me some of your golden rays so that I can spin a golden thread for the child in the manger.' And lo, when the spider descended from her web she hung on a golden thread, as strong and fine as gossamer. She landed on the hand of Mother Mary and rested happily.

Mary saw the long golden thread and said, 'Thank you good spider, with this beautiful thread I can sew a little vest for my baby'; and the spider was so pleased she climbed slowly the long way back to the web and sat there contentedly.

THE SPIDER-WEB

On the other side of the stable sat another spider in its web. Two noisy flies came buzzing in through the window in the roof of the stable. Mary and the baby were fast asleep. 'They will wake the baby,' thought the spider; and as quickly as he could he came down on a strong thread and landed lightly on the side of the manger. He spun and spun as fast as he could, from one side to the other, backwards and forwards, backwards and forwards, until he had spun a fine net over the top of the manger. Now no flies could disturb the little baby's sleep. When he was finished he quickly climbed his thread back to his web in the corner of the roof.

One of the angels, who were watching over the sleeping baby, gently touched the spider-net and it turned into fine gold.

When Mary woke and saw the beautiful golden net, she wondered where it had come from. She took a stick, which she found in the corner, and gently rolled the fine net onto it and put it away. Every night after that, she unrolled the net over the manger so that no flies would disturb the baby's sleep.

THE MOUSE

And what was the little mouse doing? When the cooing of the doves woke it, it looked around in surprise, for the stable was full of light. 'What are these strange noises in the manger?' wondered the mouse, and went to have a look. It stood on its hind legs and sniffed the strange smells with its sharp little nose. Then it dug its little claws into Mary's blue cloak and climbed into her lap.

Mary was glad that the little mouse was not afraid of her, and she sat still and spoke very softly. 'Dear little mouse, do you want to know who is lying in the manger? It is the little child of God who has been born for eternal happiness of man and animal, for all of nature, for heaven and earth. Come, I will show you the little child who has been born to bring love to the earth.'

She gently took the little mouse in her hand and held it above the child. The little mouse looked happily into the manger and squeaked 'Piep – piep, what a beautiful baby, but oh dear, it has not even a warm nest such as I always make for my babies. Oh, if only I knew how to make a warm nest for this wonderful child, it is too cold for him to lie like this, the hay is much too rough for his skin.'

And Mother Mary said, 'Dear little mouse, you have a good and sympathetic heart, and my child will remember your goodness. I will wrap him in a warm blanket, for you are right, it is too cold for him like this.'

Mary put the little mouse carefully on the ground, and it scampered away happily, probably to tell his family all about it.

THE LITTLE GLOW WORM

A little beetle overheard the angels telling the shepherds in the field that the holy child was born and lying in the manger, and he was very excited and quickly made his way to the stable. He crawled into the straw of the crib and an angel who was bending over the child saw him and said 'What are you doing here, little beetle? Please go to the animals in the field and tell them that a heavenly child has come to the earth'. 'Who will believe me?' asked the little beetle, 'I am so ugly and small.' The angel smiled and stroked the back of the beetle, and as he did so, the beetle began to shine and shine. 'Here, now you carry a light which will show them that you tell the truth,' said the angel.

Full of joy the glow-worm beetle buzzed out of the stable to the hare in the field and deer in the forest, it crawled between stones to the snail and hedgehog. It flew into the trees to the sleeping birds and called all the time: 'A heavenly child has come to the earth, a heavenly child has come to the earth.' In this way the animals learned about the holy child, and the birds were singing long before daybreak!

THE FISHES

And who told the fishes?

At the holy hour of midnight, shooting stars fell into all the waters of the world. In this way the fishes learned that it was a special night and the heavenly child had been born on earth; and from that time onwards their scales shone more beautifully than before, and reflected the stars as they swam through the waters of the sea.

The Story of the Rosebush

On a cold winter's night a rosebush lay sleeping outside a little stable. All its leaves were gone and no flowers bloomed, not even one little bud was left, it was fast asleep.

Suddenly the rosebush felt a warm glow flowing right down into its branches. It put out a few trembling green buds to feel the air, yes, it was definitely warmer! Can it be springtime? it wondered. As the rosebush opened its eyes it saw a bright light shining from the stable and wondered if it was the sun shining; and if so, how did it get inside the stable? No, it can't be, it thought, the stars are twinkling in the sky so perhaps it is the light from that bright star shining straight above me! The rosebush stretched and stretched to try to see inside the stable door, and the warmth from inside the stable made its branches tingle so much that out burst little green leaves, unfolding in the starlight.

Crunch, crunch, crunch, it heard, and three shepherds came walking towards the stable, their big boots crunching in the snow; and they stopped outside the stable door.

One carried some fur, another some wool and the third a little lamb as white as snow. They knocked at the stable door and entered, and while the door stood open the little rosebush saw that the bright light radiated from a manger in which a baby lay asleep, and next to him stood his mother who was so beautiful that the rosebush could not stop gazing at her face.

The rosebush saw how the shepherds bowed low before the manger and gave their gifts for the little child to his mother, before leaving the stable. 'Oh I so want to give that baby a gift too,' it thought; and the rosebush felt such love in its heart for the little child that this love spread out into its branches, and all of a sudden little red roses bloomed all over it. 'How can I give these roses to the child when my roots are stuck so firmly in the ground?' The rosebush asked.

Then suddenly the heavenly singing, which had been there all the while, became louder, and little fairies appeared thinking also that spring had arrived. They joined in the heavenly singing and as they flew toward the stable they stopped in surprise to see roses blooming outside in winter. 'Stop,' cried the rosebush, 'take some of my roses with you to give to the child, for I too would like to give him a gift.' The fairies each plucked a rose and carried these inside, placing them around the manger, filling the air with beautiful rose perfume.

The fairies all kissed the little child with their fairy kisses, and away they flew. Mother Mary picked up a perfect rose, and placed it in the crib, then she went outside the stable door straight to the little rosebush, touched it gently and said 'Thank you'. The rosebush shivered with happiness and each day a new rose bloomed specially for the holy child.

The Story of the Three Kings

There was once a beautiful castle in which a king lived. His name was King Melchior, and he was as kind as he was good. One night he decided to go up into the tallest tower of his castle so that he could look at the stars, which seemed to be shining more brightly than ever. He took with him a golden cup, for when he looked into this cup he could see pictures of the stars reflected.

That night he held his cup in such a way that he saw the stars, and the stars formed a crown... a crown around the head of a mother. She wore a cloak as blue as the heavens and held a child on her knee. And as the kind King Melchior looked into his cup, he saw that she beckoned to him, and he knew that he must go to her. 'But how will I find you?' he asked, and as the picture of the mother faded from the cup a great shining star appeared, and he looked up to see it shining in the heavens, and knew that he must follow that star.

Melchior called his men to bring the camels, and he put on his gold crown and his red cloak. In his hands he held a box carrying only the finest gold to take to the little child who had been born. And so kind King Melchior set out across the desert, following the star.

In another country far, far away lived wise King Balthazar. In his castle he had a grand hall with a most wonderful ceiling. This ceiling could roll back and open the room to the stars. King Balthazar loved to sit in his hall with the ceiling rolled back, and watch the smoke from the frankincense curl upwards and drift out of the roof towards the stars. Often he could see pictures in the smoke from the sweet-smelling herb.

One night he rolled back the ceiling, and the stars shone more brightly and beautifully than before. As he looked at the smoke from the sweet-smelling frankincense drifting towards the stars, he saw in the smoke a mother with a cloak as blue as the heavens. A shining crown of stars twinkled in her hair, and on her knee a child beckoned to him. 'How will I find you?' asked King Balthazar. 'Follow the star,' said the mother, and the picture faded. As he looked up, he saw a star shining so brightly in the heavens that he knew it must be the one he must follow.

Wise King Balthazar brought a jewelled box filled with frankincense, put on his beautiful blue cloak, called his men to bring the horses and rode over the fields to follow the star.

In another land lived a king called Caspar. In the gardens of his palace was a deep well, in the waters of which he could see the stars reflected. But in his country it had not rained in a long, long time and there was so little water that the only plants that grew were in his garden, and they were bushes of myrrh. People came from all around, for when they had been hurt or were in pain, the good King Caspar made an ointment from the bushes of myrrh which could heal them.

Each night he knelt by the well (for it was the only one with water still left in it) and prayed for rain to come. One night as he knelt by the well, he saw stars reflected in the water. They shone so brightly that they dazzled his eyes, and from the middle of the stars emerged the picture of a mother with a cloak as blue as the heavens, and a crown of stars around her head. On her knees sat a child who beckoned to him. 'How do I find you?' he asked, and the mother pointed to a star which shone brighter than all the others, and he knew he must follow that star. All of a sudden drops began to fall into the well, the picture of the mother disappeared and the rain fell, watering the parched earth. King Caspar knew that his prayers had been answered. The old king put branches of the healing myrrh into a box, put on his green cloak, and set off on his journey, always following the star.

For many days the three kings travelled until they met in the desert, and then all three together followed the star until it stopped above a stable. In the stable sat a mother with a child on her knee, and her cloak was as blue as the heavens, and in her hair was a crown of stars. Around the child light glowed and the kings knew that he must be the newborn king. They took off their crowns before him, and knelt down on the floor.

'Greetings to thee, child so fair, gold I bring to thee,' said the good King Melchior. 'Greetings to thee, child so rare, frankincense I bring to thee,' said the kind King Balthazar. 'Greetings to thee, child so dear, healing myrrh I bring to thee,' said the wise King Caspar. They bowed before the little child, and gave their gifts to his mother who thanked them graciously. The child raised his hand and smiled gently at the three kings, who quietly left the stall.

As they left the stable they marvelled at all they had seen, and that such a child who had been born in a stable could be king of all mankind, bringing joy and love to the world.

Appendix 1:
Costumes and Props

MARY:
Red dress
Mid-blue veil
Crown of stars (for Three Kings play)

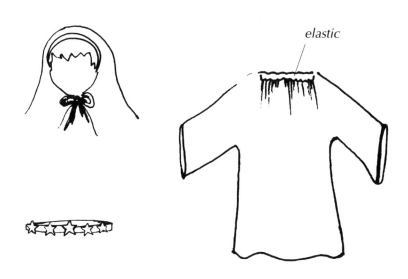

elastic

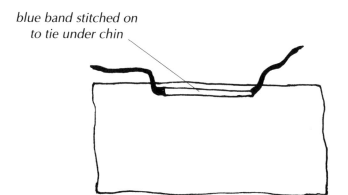

*blue band stitched on
to tie under chin*

JOSEPH:
Brown robe (as Mary's dress)
Beard if possible
Hat or cloth headdress

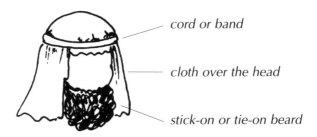

cord or band

cloth over the head

stick-on or tie-on beard

OX:
Brown robe or cloak
Brown cap with horns

*brown material sewn around
wire and stitched onto cap*

DONKEY:
Grey robe or cloak
Grey cap with ears

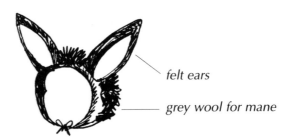

felt ears

grey wool for mane

ANGEL WHO BRINGS BABY:
White dress with wings
Gold headband

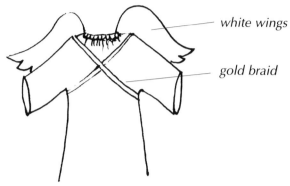

white wings

gold braid

STAR-ANGEL:
White dress with veil
Crown with star

soft white muslin pinned
over dress

SHEPHERDS:
As Joseph
Shirts and jerkins

KINGS:
Red, green and blue cloaks
Crowns
Shiny robes

*gold card, or spray
with gold paint*

elastic

KINGS' SERVANTS:
Cloaks

RABBITS:
Outfits as illustrated
or simply caps with ears

GNOMES:
Brown dresses or cloaks
Caps with fur beards

fur beard sewn on to cap

CUCKOO AND PIGEON:
Coloured dresses
Wing veils
Feathered crowns

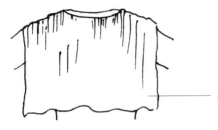

coloured muslin

FAIRIES:
Coloured dresses
Wings

elastic to fit around wrist

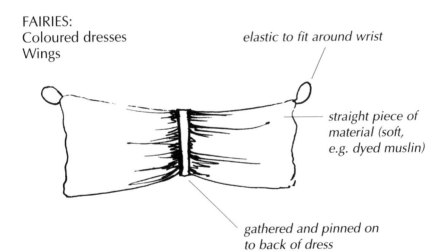

straight piece of material (soft, e.g. dyed muslin)

gathered and pinned on to back of dress

ROSEBUSH:
Green dress
Rose crown

STABLE:
Manger with straw and a small blanket to cover the baby
2 small stools for Mary and Joseph
A hook to hang the lantern

BABY JESUS:
A small soft doll about nine inches long. Unformed features
(eyes and mouth only). Wrapped in a pale pink/peach or yellow
silk material, tied around with a gold thread.

LANTERN:
Cardboard lantern cutout with base
Candle in centre and wire handle

STARS/ANGELS:
Gold stars on top of gold-painted sticks
Bells

SHEPHERDS' GIFTS:
Piece of sheepskin/fur
Fleece
White toy lamb

KINGS' GIFTS:
Stone sprayed gold in open container
Stick of incense in an elaborate jar or painted bottle
Herb in a small ornate box

JOSEPH:
Wooden staff

ROSEBUSH:
Tissue roses on sticks
Basket

Appendix 2: Making the Figures

THE FIGURES

Hammer a large nail (approximately 10cm long) into the centre of a piece of cut-off dowel (approximately 3cm thick).

The sizes of the figures can be varied by making the dowel longer or shorter.

Wrap a pipe cleaner or wire around the nail and turn back the ends.

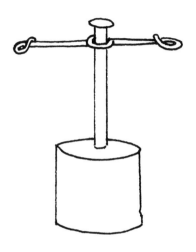

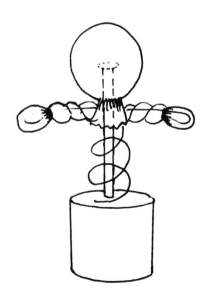

Make a head from a piece of stockinette (or old dyed t-shirt or vest material) tied over a ball of wool or kapok.

Wind material around the arms and tie in place with cotton thread.

More material can be wound around the nail and glued to the dowel to make a thicker and more solid body.

Hair of different kinds and colours of wool can be glued or
sewn on.

Soft features – eyes and mouth only – can be drawn on with
coloured pencils.

The figures can be dressed according to the indications given for
the costumes.

Stabilise by gluing the base of the dowel onto a piece of round
cardboard.

THE BABY

Make the head out of stockinette tied at the neck over kapok or wool, and wrap in silky swaddling clothes (pale yellow or peach, sewed or glued together and tied with gold thread).

Hair can be glued on or the silk cloth can be wrapped around the head.

 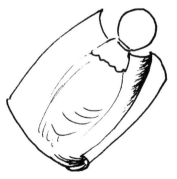

OX AND DONKEY

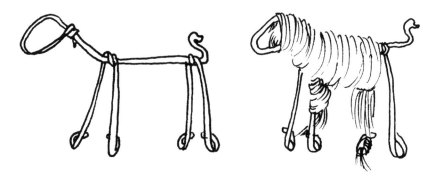

The bodies may be shaped out of pipe cleaners and wound with thick brown or grey carded or rough natural wool.

You can bend the ears to shape, or turn them into horns for the ox and glue on felt ears.

The sheep can be made in the same way, and the legs bent under to make them lie down.

The donkey can also be sewn from felt. Cut two sides and one underneath piece and sew together, stuff with wool or kapok. Add ears, mane and tail.

 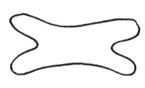

SHEEP

The sheep can be made in two ways, either by wrapping wool around smaller pipe cleaners in the same way as the Ox and Donkey (above) or by making them out of pompoms.

POMPOM SHEEP

Make two pom-poms by cutting two pieces of card the same size (fig 1 and 2).

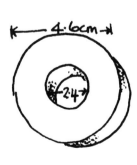 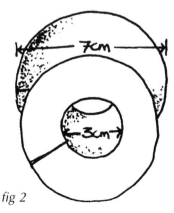

fig 1   fig 2

Loop a strong piece of wool twice around the centre hole on one of the cardboard rings, and lay the second ring of the same size on top of it. Let the ends of the loop hang down outside the rings and take care not to cut them off. (fig 3)

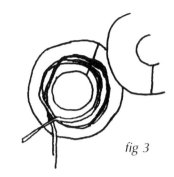

fig 3

Choose suitable colour wool and wind loosely round the rings until the hole in the centre is full. (fig 4)

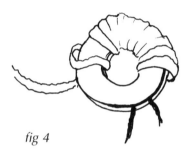

fig 4

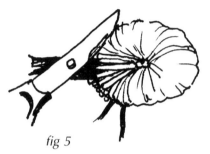

fig 5

Push a scissor between the two rings and cut the wool around the outside. (fig 5) Pull the loop of wool which was laid between the rings tight, and tie it firmly. (leave long)

Carefully remove the cardboard rings. Trim the pompom.

Make the smaller pompom in the same way and tie the two together with the loose loop threads. Glue on the ears to the smaller pompom. (fig 6)

fig 6

Appendix 3: Making the Advent Calendar

YOU WILL NEED:
1 pipe cleaner (or thin wire) about 30cm long
1 pipe cleaner about 15cm long
Piece of white or pale yellow silk about 32 cm x 16 cm
(or other thin material such as muslin)
Length of carded wool (fleece) or cotton wool
Small length pale yellow/light-brown carded wool (or soft
    mohair) for hair
White cotton thread
Gold thread
Small gold star
Gold cardboard

fig 1

THE ANGEL

Fold long pipe cleaner in half with a
loop for the head in the centre and twist.
(fig 1) Twist a small loop at each end of
the short pipe cleaner and wrap the
centre around the 'head' wire.

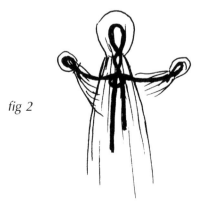

fig 2

Pull a piece of fleece off
the length and fold over
the loop of the pipe
cleaner forming a head
about the size of a large
marble; leave a length of
fleece to form the 'body'
under the silk. Tie loosely
with cotton. Do the same
around each 'hand'. (fig 2)

Fold the silk in half lengthways to form a square 16cm x 16cm and cut the corners off the silk as illustrated. (fig 3)

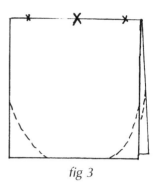

fig 3

Open the silk and place the centre over the 'head'. Wind the gold thread around the neck a few times and tie securely. Tie the hands about 3cm in at each end of the fold of the silk in the same way. (fig 4)

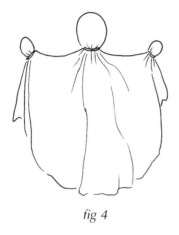

fig 4

Pull into shape and arrange the face and hands.

Arrange the dress so that it falls into nice folds.

Glue the yellow wool to the head and cut to required length. Tie the gold thread around the head of the angel and glue the tiny star to the centre of the forehead.

Cut the wings from the gold card (fig 5a) and place a large paperclip in the centre. (fig 5b)

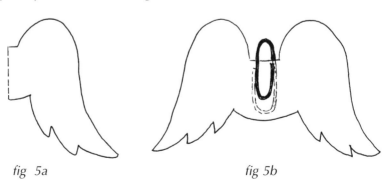

fig 5a   *fig 5b*

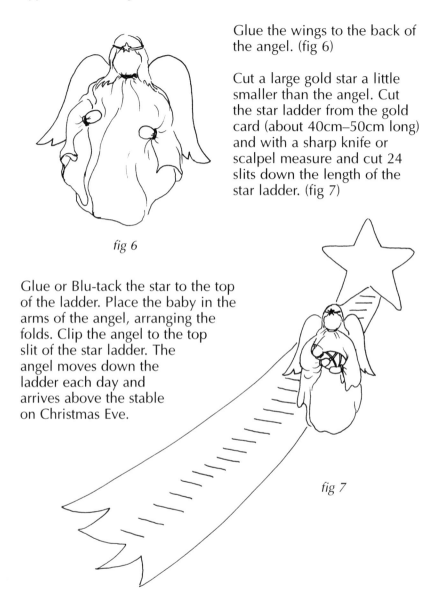

Glue the wings to the back of the angel. (fig 6)

Cut a large gold star a little smaller than the angel. Cut the star ladder from the gold card (about 40cm–50cm long) and with a sharp knife or scalpel measure and cut 24 slits down the length of the star ladder. (fig 7)

fig 6

Glue or Blu-tack the star to the top of the ladder. Place the baby in the arms of the angel, arranging the folds. Clip the angel to the top slit of the star ladder. The angel moves down the ladder each day and arrives above the stable on Christmas Eve.

fig 7

On Christmas Day the baby 'appears' in the manger and the angel can either hang from a branch or stand next to the stable. The star ladder has gone and the gold star appears above the stable.

Appendix 4:
Music and Songs

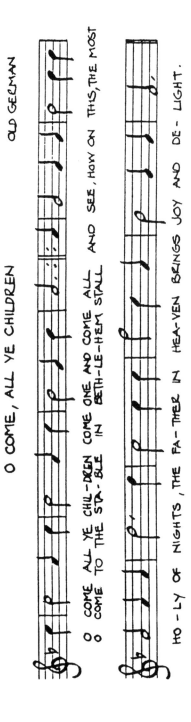

O COME, ALL YE CHILDREN

OLD GERMAN

O COME ALL YE CHIL-DREN COME ONE AND COME ALL AND SEE, HOW ON THIS, THE MOST

O COME TO THE STA-BLE IN BETH-LE-HEM STALL

HO-LY OF NIGHTS, THE FA-THER IN HEA-VEN BRINGS JOY AND DE-LIGHT.

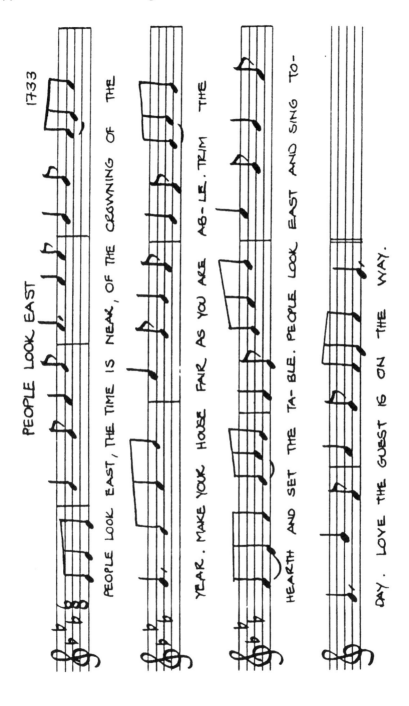

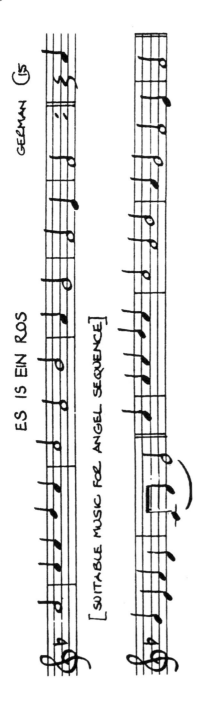

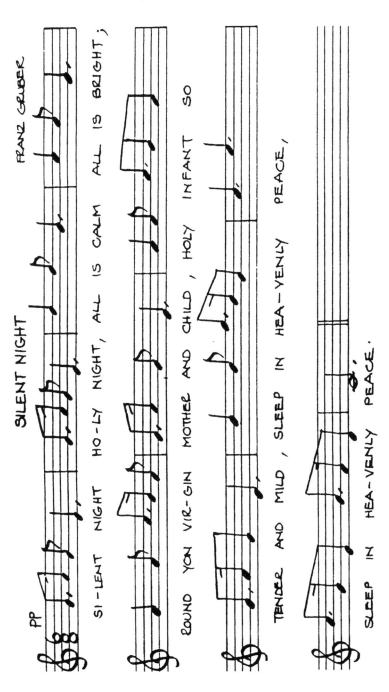

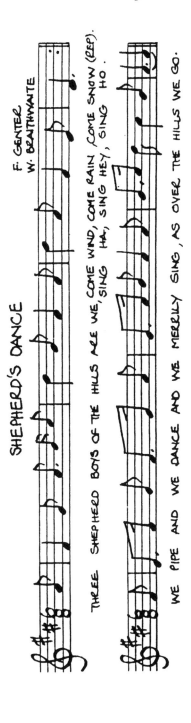

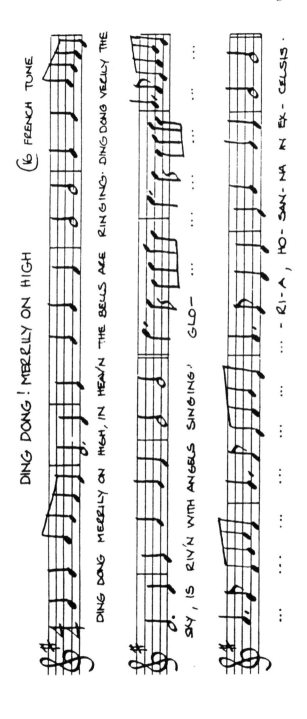

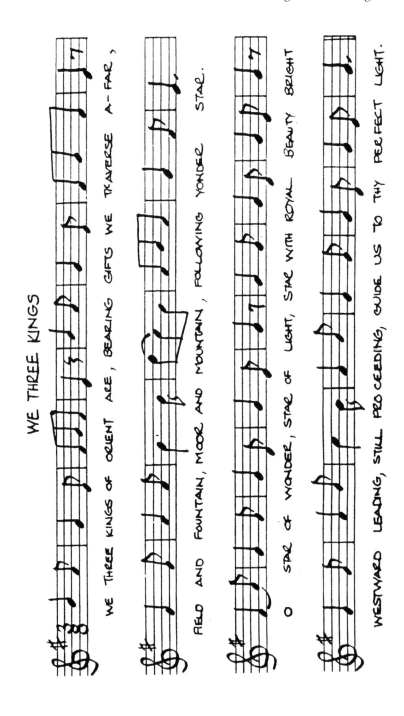

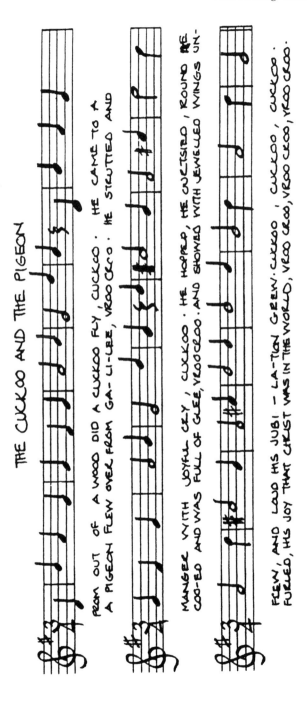

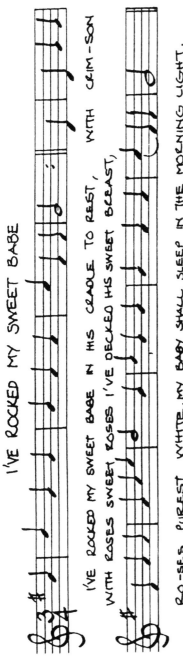

WE ARE THE CLEVER LITTLE GNOMES

WE ARE THE CLEVER LITTLE GNOMES, THE CRAGGY MOUNTAINS WITH HAM-MER STRONG WE KNOCK-KNOCK-KNOCK, AGAINST THE SOLID

ARE OUR HOMES, WE WORK FROM MORN 'TILL NIGHT. ROCK, ROCK, ROCK, TO SEEK FOR TREASURES BRIGHT.

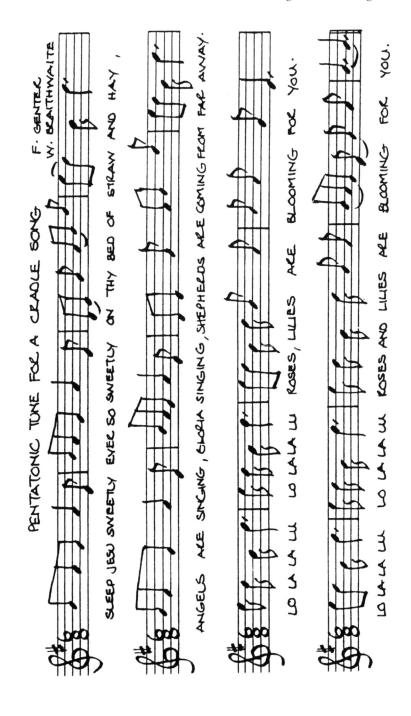

A NEW BOOK OF NEW (AND RE-TOLD) SHORT
CHRISTMAS STORIES, PARTICULARLY SUITABLE FOR
CHILDREN FROM TWO TO NINE YEARS OLD,
IS ALSO AVAILABLE TO ACCOMPANY THIS BOOK.

Christmas Stories Together

Estelle Bryer and Janni Nicol

Illustrated by Marije Rowling

PUBLISHED BY HAWTHORN PRESS

128pp; 210 x 148mm; paperback; 1 903 458 22 6

About the Authors

ESTELLE BRYER

Estelle Bryer, a founder teacher of the Waldorf School, Constantia, Cape Town, has been there for 42 years as kindergarten teacher, eurythmy teacher and eurythmy therapist. She specialises in kindergarten eurythmy.

She has lectured widely to diverse audiences, teacher training centres and professional groups. She is also a published author of children's stories and puppet plays.

Estelle is best known as South Africa's foremost puppeteer for children, having performed solo to more than three quarters of a million children and adults over the past 38 years. She established the only permanent puppet theatre in the country, which performs weekly to the public. She is also Janni's mother.

JANNI NICOL

Janni Nicol trained as a Steiner kindergarten teacher in 1969. Since then she taught in various kindergartens, and helped to found the Rosebridge Kindergarten and Cambridge Steiner School, UK. She has worked in marketing and PR, published articles and become a puppeteer. She is also Early Years Representative for the Steiner Waldorf Schools Fellowship, UK.

She has lectured on many aspects of Steiner education, multiculturalism and puppetry. This is her first book with her mother Estelle Bryer.

Other books from Hawthorn Press

Storytelling with Children
Nancy Mellon

Telling stories awakens wonder and creates special
occasions with children, whether it is bedtime,
around the fire or on rainy days. Nancy Mellon
shows how you can become a confident storyteller
and enrich your family with the power of story.
192pp; 216 x 138mm; illustrations; paperback;
1 903458 08 0

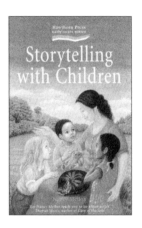

Free to Learn
Introducing Steiner Waldorf early
childhood education
Lynne Oldfield

Free to Learn is a unique guide to the principles and
methods of Steiner Waldorf early childhood
education. This authoritative introduction is written
by Lynne Oldfield, Director of the London Steiner
Waldorf Early Childhood Teacher Training course.
She draws on kindergarten experience from around
the world, with stories, helpful insights, lively
observations and pictures. This inspiring book will
interest parents, educators and early years students.
It is up to date, comprehensive, includes many
photos and has a 16 page colour section.
256pp; 216 x 138mm; photographs; paperback; 1 903458 06 4

Star and Planet Almanac 2002
A monthly guide to the sky at night
Liesbeth Bisterbosch

Find your way around the night skies in 2002 with these beautiful astronomical charts! Stargazers can navigate the heavens easily with this hand companion guide. You can track the paths of the planets, locate the constellations and see meteor showers. This practical guide to naked eye astronomy will help you keep in touch with the movements of the planets around the year.
16pp; 426 x 293mm; paperback; 1 903458 13 7

Free Range Education
How home education works
Terri Dowty (ed)

Welcome to this essential handbook for families
considering or starting out in home education.
Free Range Education is full of family stories,
resources, burning questions, humour, tips,
practical steps and useful advice so you can
choose what best suits your family situation. You
are already your child's main teacher and these
families show how home education can work for
you. Both parents and children offer useful
guidance, based on their experience.
256pp; 210 x 148mm; cartoons; paperback; 1 903458 07 2

The Genius of Play
Celebrating the spirit of childhood
Sally Jenkinson

Children move like quick fire from the fantastic to
the everyday, when free to express the genius of play.
The Genius of Play addresses what play is, why it
matters, and how modern life endangers children's
play. The secrets of play are explored from moving
stories and research. Here is an outspoken Children's
Play Charter for parents and teachers, which
celebrates the playful spirit of childhood.
224pp; 216 x 138mm; paperback; 1 903458 04 8

'A beautiful and important book.'
Mary Jane Drummond, University of Cambridge

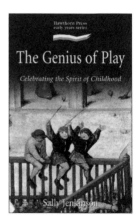

All Year Round
Ann Druitt, Christine Fynes-Clinton,
Marije Rowling

All Year Round is brimming with things to make; activities, stories, poems and songs to share with your family. It is full of well illustrated ideas for fun and celebration: from Candlemas to Christmas and Midsummer's day to the Winter solstice. Observing the round of festivals is an enjoyable way to bring rhythm into children's lives and provide a series of meaningful landmarks to look forward to. Each festival has a special character of its own: participation can deepen our understanding and love of nature and bring a gift to the whole family.
320pp; 250 x 200mm; drawings; paperback; 1 869 890 47 7

Festivals, Family and Food
Diana Carey and Judy Large

A source of stories, recipes, things to make, activities, poems, songs and festivals. Each festival such as Christmas, Candlemas and Martinmas has its own, well illustrated chapter. There are also sections on Birthdays, Rainy Days, Convalescence and a birthday Calendar. The perfect present for a family, it explores the numerous festivals that children love celebrating.

224pp; 250 x 200mm; illustrations; paperback; 0 950 706 23 X

Festivals Together
A guide to multicultural celebration
*Sue Fitzjohn, Minda Weston,
Judy Large*

This special book for families and teachers
helps you celebrate festivals from cultures
from all over the world. This resource guide
for celebration introduces a selection of 26
Buddhist, Christian, Hindu, Jewish, Muslim
and Sikh festivals. It offers a lively introduction to the wealth of different ways of
life. There are stories, things to make,
recipes, songs, customs and activities for
each festival, comprehensively illustrated.
224pp; 250 x 200mm; illustrations;
paperback; 1 869 890 46 9

The Children's Year
Crafts and clothes for children and parents to make
Stephanie Cooper, Christine Fynes-Clinton, Marije Rowling

You needn't be an experienced craftsperson
to create beautiful things! This step by step,
well illustrated book with clear instructions
shows you how to get started. Children and
parents are encouraged to try all sorts of
handwork, with different projects relating to
the seasons of the year.

Here are soft toys, wooden toys, moving toys such as balancing birds or
climbing gnomes, horses, woolly hats, mobiles and dolls. There are over 100
treasures to make in seasonal groupings around the children's year.
192pp; 250 x 200mm; paperback; 1 869 890 00 0

Games Children Play
How games and sport help children develop
Kim Brooking-Payne
Illustrated by Marije Rowling

Games Children Play offers an accessible
guide to games with children of age 3
upwards. These games are all tried and tested,
and are the basis for the author's extensive
teacher training work.

The book explores children's personal development and how this is expressed
in movement, play, songs and games. Each game is clearly and simply
described, with diagrams or drawings, and accompanied by an explanation of
why this game is helpful at a particular age. The equipment that may be
needed is basic, cheap and easily available.
192pp; 297 x 210mm; paperback; 1 869 890 78 7

Muddles, Puddles and Sunshine
Your activity book to help when someone has died
Winston's Wish

Muddles, Puddles and Sunshine
offers practical and sensitive
support for bereaved children.
Beautifully illustrated in colour,
it suggests a helpful series of
activities and exercises
accompanied by the friendly
characters of Bee and Bear.

32pp; 297 x 210mm landscape; illustrations; paperback; 1 869 890 58 2

Pull the Other One!
String Games and Stories Book 1
Michael Taylor

This well-travelled and entertaining series of tales
is accompanied by clear instructions and
explanatory diagrams – guaranteed not to tie you
in knots and will teach you tricks with which to
dazzle your friends! With something for everyone,
these ingenious tricks and tales are developed and
taught with utter simplicity, making them suitable
from age 5 upwards.
128pp; 216 x 148mm; drawings; paperback;
1 869 890 49 3

Kinder Dolls
A Waldorf doll-making handbook
Maricristin Sealey

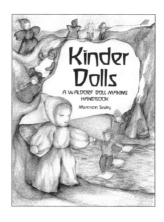

Kinder Dolls shows how to create handcrafted
dolls from natural materials. A range of simple,
colourful designs will inspire both beginners
and experienced doll makers alike. These dolls
are old favourites, originating in Waldorf
Steiner kindergartens where parents make dolls
together for their children, and for the school.
160pp; 246 x 189mm; drawings; paperback;
1 903458 03 X

*'Maricristin's book is a fine source for the beginner doll maker. It is a valuable
primer, full of practical tips, simple designs and clear, easy to follow instructions.*
Sara McDonald,
Magic Cabin Dolls

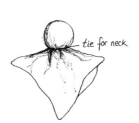

Beyond the Forest
The Story of Parsifal and the Grail
Kelvin Hall

The Grail Quest is an archetypal story of the journey of humanity and of each person. Parsifal's search for wholeness – passed down by generations of storytellers – is re-told vividly here by Kelvin Hall.

There is a Parsifal is every one of us as we move from the innocence and naivety of forgetting, through courage and surrender, to love and redemption. Impaired by fear, bewilderment, loss and misunderstanding, we learn to trust the instinct of the heart as well as accepting the wisdom and support of others on the way.

This ancient story, told by Wolfram von Eschenbach in the Middle Ages, asks us why we restrain ourselves from asking the compassionate question. It shows how the result is our suffering and alienation, and that by engaging with the suffering of others, we acknowledge our own. This brings forth the possibility for transformation and renewal.

'The story of Parsifal is close to my heart, and Kelvin Hall's gift is to bring it closer to all of ours in a language that can truly speak to us now.'
Jay Ramsay

Because this is an initiation story, it will be especially useful to English and Drama teachers, storytellers and psychotherapists. This Parsifal story is an essential part of the Steiner/Waldorf curriculum for Class 11 (17 year olds) and *Beyond the Forest* is the most accessible version for teenagers.

Kelvin Hall was first told the Parsifal story by his future wife, Barbara. Storyteller-in-residence at Ruskin Mill, Gloucestershire, he is well-known on the festival circuit. He won the Hodja Cup for Lying at the Crick Crack Club, 1st April 1993.

96pp; 216 x 138mm; 1 869 890 73 6

Troll of Tree Hill
Judy Large
Illustrations by Tom Nelson

We have all heard about
children who do not believe
in fairies or trolls. Here is a
story about a troll who does
not believe in children. With
his age-old hatred of
humankind, how will Troll
handle the sudden invasion of
his woodland home?
72pp; 210 x 297 mm; paperback; 1 869 890 74 4

Told by the Peat Fire
Sybille Alexander

The voice behind these much loved Celtic tales is the
passionate voice of a true storyteller – it crackles with
humour and ancient wisdom as it lifts the veil
between us and the spiritual world. These are
universal stories of power and laughter offering as
much hope and reassurance to the listeners of today
as they did through the long nights of winters past.
128pp; 216 x 138 mm; paperback; 1 869 890 23 X

*'At the heart of these wonderful stories is the passion of a true storyteller.
Sibylle Alexander has the gift, the energy and the vivid imagination to make the
words of her tales sing.'*
Dr Donald Smith, Director of the Scottish Storytelling Centre

The Green Snake and the Beautiful Lily
Johann Wolfgang von Goethe
Play Version – Michael Burton
Original Translation of the Fairy Tale – Thomas Carlyle
The Art of Goethean Conversation – Marjorie Spock

A group of people live in a world turned upside down. They realise that the efforts of one alone can do little to create a new society. But by waking up to each other at the right time, they bring about profound spiritual and social renewal.

Goethe originally told this magic tale in a group of travellers during the French Revolution. Today, this magic still sparkles in Thomas Carlyle's original translation.

Michael Burton's play invites you to enjoy the tale afresh through his punchy dialogue. Jay Ramsay writes that this, '... *inspiring script is a genuine contribution, combining the grace of the original fairy tale with a brilliant use of the modern idiom*'

And when the Green Snake is asked by the Gold King, 'What is more quickening than light?' she replies, 'Conversation!' We come alive when meeting each other in real dialogue. Marjorie Spock's Art of Goethean Conversation shows how true conversation has transformative power.

This book was published specially for the 1998-99 European Tour of the Mask Studio's production of *The Green Snake,* a new play inspired by Goethe's fairy tale. It also meets readers' requests for the Spock essay and Carlyle translation in an accessible form.

96pp; 216 x 138mm; paperback; 1 869 890 07 8

Sing Me the Creation
Paul Matthews

This is an inspirational workbook of creative writing exercises for poets and teachers, and for all who wish to develop the life of the imagination. There are over 300 exercises for improving writing skills. Though intended for group work with adults, teachers will find these exercises easily adaptable to the classroom. Paul Matthews, a poet himself, taught creative writing at Emerson College, Sussex.
224pp; 238 x 135mm; 1 869 890 60 4;

Naming
Choosing a meaningful name
Caroline Sherwood

Names matter. They are the fingerprints of the Soul through which we express our nature to the world. Choosing a meaningful name is a lifetime gift. Included in this thorough, authoritative, and fascinating book is everything you need to choose, or change, a name and plan a naming ceremony.
304pp; 246 x 189 mm; paperback;
1 869 890 56 6

Rosie Styles, of The Baby Naming Society, has written the Foreword for this extensive and insightful book, and says:
'Caroline Sherwood's Naming *is a completely new and far more useful approach in which the meanings of names are the prime focus. With a deep respect for language, she offers a fresh way for parents to set about finding the right name for their child. This is a much needed addition to the naming books already available, and will delight anyone facing the enormous task of naming their child, or those with an interest in names.'*

Getting in touch with Hawthorn Press

We would be delighted to hear your feedback on our Festivals books, how they can be improved, and what your needs are. Visit our website for details of the Festivals Series and forthcoming books and events: **http://www.hawthornpress.com**

Ordering books

If you have difficulties ordering Hawthorn Press books from a bookshop, you can order direct from:

United Kingdom
  Scottish Book Source Distribution,
  137 Dundee Street, Edinburgh,
  EH11 1BG
  Tel: 0131 229 6800 Fax: 0131 229 9070

North America
  Anthroposophic Press c/o Books International,
  PO Box 960,
  Herndon, VA 201 72-0960.
  Toll free order line: 800-856-8664
  Toll free fax line: 800-277-9747

Dear Reader

If you wish to follow up your reading of this book, please tick the boxes below as appropriate, fill in your name and address and return to Hawthorn Press:

☐ Please send me a catalogue of other Hawthorn Press books.

☐ Please send me details of 'Festivals' events and courses.

My feedback about 'Festivals':

Name _____

Address _____

_____

_____

Postcode _____ Tel. no. _____

Please return to: Hawthorn Press, Hawthorn House,
1 Lansdown Lane, Stroud, Glos. GL5 1BJ, UK
or Fax (01453) 751135

cct